Reflections Within

Navigating the Depths of Self Through Poetry

Talia Quell

In the quiet spaces between breaths and the tumultuous rhythms of daily life, there exists a profound depth of understanding and connection waiting to be discovered. This collection of poems, crafted with the intent to explore the vast landscapes of human emotion and experience, serves as a gateway to such discoveries. Within these pages, readers are invited to embark on a journey—a journey that meanders through the valleys of self-discovery, soars over the peaks of resilience, and rests in the fields of mindfulness and presence.

Each poem is a reflection, a moment captured in the dance of words, offering insights into the art of letting go, the celebration of individuality, and the embrace of change. They are verses that challenge the notion of fitting into a pre-defined mold, encouraging the reader to appreciate the quirks and nuances that make each journey unique. Through the rhythm of rhyme and the freedom of free verse, this collection seeks to validate and celebrate the individual paths we tread in the pursuit of understanding ourselves and the world around us.

The themes woven throughout these poems—ranging from the introspective exploration of self-forgiveness to the outward expression of self-empowerment—serve as a reminder of the strength found in vulnerability, the beauty in personal growth, and the peace in present-mindedness. It is a call to recognize and honor the complexity of the human spirit, with all its flaws and fancies.

As you turn these pages, may you find solace in the shared experience of searching for meaning, comfort in the commonality of life's struggles, and joy in the celebration of your own individuality. This book is not just a collection of poems but an invitation to reflect, to pause, and to appreciate the intricate tapestry of human existence.

Let this preface serve as a doorway into the world of contemplation and insight that these poems aspire to provide. In reading them, may you embark on a journey of your own, discovering along the way the myriad ways in which life unfolds in its mysterious, challenging, and often beautiful patterns. Welcome to a celebration of life, in all its forms, as we explore together the art of living deeply and truly.

Whispers of Time

In the quiet, amidst the tick-tock of the aging clock,
I found beauty in the seconds that danced away.
Time whispered tales of yesteryears and tomorrows not promised,
Teaching me the grace of now, the power of presence.
In every fleeting moment, I saw life's ephemeral beauty,
A reminder to embrace the now, for it too shall pass.
Like petals in the wind, we are but whispers of time,
Fleeting, yet forever etched in the fabric of existence.

The Fear Within

In the shadow of the night, where fears often dwell,
I found strength in confronting the darkness within.
Fear, a constant companion, whispering doubts and what-ifs,
Became the catalyst for my transformation.
Embracing the unknown, I stepped into the light,
Discovering that courage was always there, quietly waiting.
For in facing our fears, we uncover the power to rise,
To become the architects of our destiny, unchained and free.

The Dance of Empathy

In the silent language of the heart, empathy speaks,
A tender dance of souls, connecting without words.
Your joy, my joy; your pain, my sorrow;
A shared journey through the highs and lows of life.
Empathy, the bridge between worlds,
Teaching us the beauty of understanding,
And in this dance, we find the essence of love,
A reminder that in feeling for another, we become truly human.

The Garden of Self

In the garden of self, where thoughts bloom like flowers,
I discovered the seeds of self-esteem, deep within.
Watered by acceptance, nurtured by love's gentle touch,
They grew, roots entwining with the essence of my being.
Self-worth, a delicate bloom, unfurling in the sunlight,
Teaching me that love starts with the self,
A reflection of the beauty within,
A testament to the power of nurturing one's own soul.

Mirror, Mirror

Mirror, mirror, on the wall,
Show me the truth behind the fall.
Not of beauty, nor of grace,
But of the light within my space.
For self-esteem, like glass so clear,
Reflects the love we hold dear.
And in this reflection, I find my worth,
Rooted deep within the earth.
For to love and be loved, in return,
Is the greatest lesson we can learn.

The Architect of Self

I am the architect of my own esteem,
Building foundations on dreams and self-belief.
With every brick laid in confidence and grace,
I construct a sanctuary, a sacred place.
Self-worth, the cornerstone of this edifice,
Supports the structure of my happiness.
For in recognizing our own intrinsic value,
We find the strength to face life anew.

Echoes of Worth

In the quiet moments, I hear the echoes of my worth,
A gentle reminder of my place on this Earth.
Not measured by accolades or external acclaim,
But by the love I give, and the spirits I tame.
For self-esteem is not a prize to be won,
But a journey, a race that's never done.
It's in the striving, the reaching for the stars,
That we find our value, and heal our scars.

The Light Within

There's a light within each of us, so bright and so warm,
A beacon of self-esteem, through every storm.
It guides us to love, to be loved in kind,
In its glow, our true selves we find.
For the roots of self-worth lie in knowing our light,
Embracing our power, our own unique sight.
In this light, we are unbound, free,
Masters of our destiny, as we were meant to be.

The Uncharted Path

On the uncharted path of self-discovery,
I wander, a seeker of the depths within.
Each step, a question; each turn, a lesson,
Unveiling the layers of my soul's skin.
Not in the echoes of others' voices
But in the silence, I find my choices.
A journey not of miles, but of inner space,
Where love and self-worth interlace.

The Reflection

In the quiet waters of contemplation,
I saw myself, a reflection anew.
Not the image the world wished to see,
But my essence, raw and true.
In this mirror of introspection,
Lies the power of self-direction.
Understanding my identity,
Unlocks the doors to my own infinity.

The Tapestry

Life, a tapestry of woven threads,
Each color a belief, a value held dear.
In the weaving, I discover
The patterns of my soul, crystal clear.
With every thread of love and worth,
I craft my identity, my own earth.
A fabric rich with self-made design,
Where every strand is purely mine.

The Inner Compass

With an inner compass in my hand,
I navigate the seas of my heartland.
Through storms of doubt and waves of despair,
It guides me with a tender care.
Pointing towards true north—self-knowing,
A light in the darkness, ever glowing.
In this journey of self-discovery,
I find my essence, my own treasury.

The Phoenix's Flight

From the ashes of my former self,
A phoenix rises, in luminous stealth.
In the flames of trials, I am reborn,
A new being, no longer forlorn.
This journey of transformation,
A testament to self-realization.
In the flight of discovery, I soar,
Embracing myself, forever more.

The Paradoxes of Love and Self-Esteem

In the dance of light and shadow,
love and self-esteem entwine,
A paradox where the heart battles
between ego and the divine.
To love oneself,
a journey of acceptance and pride,
Yet, in love for another,
our own desires we often hide.
A balance sought,
on a tightrope of self and care,
Where loving truly means to give,
to support, and to share.
Yet, within this contradiction,
a beautiful truth we find,
That love, in its essence,
is both selfless and kind.

The Alchemy of Transformation

Through the crucible of love, our hearts
undergo transmutation,
Turning leaden fears into golden revelations.
The journey toward self-esteem, a path of
inner alchemy,
Where love transforms perception, and we
begin to truly see.
No longer bound by past constraints or
societal decree,
We emerge transformed, in love and self,
completely free.
This alchemy of the soul, where love and
self-regard meld,
Reveals a world anew, in every moment beheld.

Philosophical Dialogues with the Self

In the quiet of the mind, a dialogue unfolds,
Where the self debates on values, love, and roads untold.
"Is love the highest good?" one part earnestly inquires,
While another counters, "But self-love inspires."
This inner conversation, a philosophical quest,
To find where love and value in harmony rest.
A journey through the mind's own labyrinthine weave,
Seeking answers to how we love, believe, and perceive.

The Ethics of Love

In the realm of hearts, where emotions flow and merge,
Lies a complex ethics, a moral urge.
To love with integrity, respect, and care,
Balancing self-regard with the willingness to share.
What duty do we owe to ourselves,
and to the heart of another?
Can love be just, can it be fair, or does it smother?
These ethical questions, in love's vast domain,
Prompt us to consider how love and morality can coexist, sustain.

The Aesthetics of Love and Self

In love's expression, a beauty so profound,
Aesthetic reflections in every sound.
The elegance found in recognizing one's worth,
Mirrored in the love we spread upon this earth.
Each gesture, each word, a masterpiece of the heart,
A poetic ode to the art of playing one's part.
In this aesthetic journey, love and self-esteem blend,
Creating a tapestry of life, woven end to end.

Metaphysics of the Heart

What is love, if not the soul's deepest query?
A metaphysical dance, both elusive and merry.
How do love and self, in the cosmos align,
Are they but constructs, or divine by design?
This exploration of existence, of essence and esteem,
Seeks to uncover love's true regime.
In the heart's vast expanses, where feelings reside,
Lies the universe's secrets, forever to confide.

Myths, Legends, and Love

In the tapestry of myths, where heroes and gods play,
Lie tales of love, complex in their sway.
Reimagining these stories, with love at the core,
Offers new insights, philosophies to explore.
How does love shape the legend, the myth, the lore?
In its power, do we find something worth fighting for?
These ancient narratives, through love's lens seen,
Reveal timeless truths on what it means to love, to dream.

Love's Influence on Perception

Love, a prism through which reality bends,
Colors perceptions, on this it depends.
The world anew, through the eyes of the heart,
Where every end is just another start.
How does love alter our view of the self, the other?
Does it reveal truths, or reality smother?
In this philosophical inquiry, love's role we discern,
In shaping the way the world we perceive, learn.

The Healing Power of Love

In the balm of love, wounds find their salve,
Healing power in its gentle halve.
Self-acceptance, the first step on this path,
Where love's warmth bathes us, aftermath.
Through the scars and the pain, love gently weaves,
A tapestry of healing, in which the heart believes.
This poem, a testament to love's enduring might,
To mend, to heal, to bring into the light.

The Solitude of Self

In solitude's embrace, a silent song,
Where one finds strength, a place to belong.
The solitude of self, not loneliness but space,
To meet one's own gaze, to find one's own grace.
In this quietude, love and self-respect bloom,
A solitary garden, dispelling gloom.
For in the depths of solitude, we come to see,
The love for oneself sets the heart free.

Veil of Perception

Beneath the veil of perception, lies a world unseen,
Where reality and illusion in a dance convene.
What we perceive, a mere fragment of the vast unknown,
A universe beyond the senses, unshown.
In this realm of consciousness, questions arise,
What is truly real, beyond our eyes?
A quest for truth, in the mind's deep sea,
Exploring the nature of reality.

Echoes of Existence

In the silence of the cosmos, echoes of existence
resonate,
A symphony of the real, and the perceptions we create.
The physical universe, expansive and wide,
Yet bound by the limits of our human sight.
What is the fabric of this grand design,
If not interwoven threads of the divine?
Contemplating the vastness, our minds take flight,
Seeking the essence of the dark and the light.

Shadows on the Cave Wall

Like shadows on the cave wall, our reality distorts,
A reflection of the truth, in our thoughts it courts.
What we see, mere shadows of a higher plane,
Illusions that our consciousness struggles to explain.
Are we but prisoners of our own mind's cave,
Seeking the light, the truth we crave?
In this allegory of life, a philosophical quest,
To discern the real, and with wisdom, be blessed.

The Fabric of the Cosmos

The fabric of the cosmos, woven with precision and care,
A tapestry of reality, in which we all share.
But what is the thread that binds this design,
Is it material, or something divine?
The nature of reality, complex and profound,
In the quantum dance, its secrets are found.
A universe of possibilities, open and vast,
In the nature of reality, our future is cast.

Mirrors of the Mind

In the mirrors of the mind, reality bends,
A labyrinth of perceptions, where beginning meets end.
What is real, if not a construct of thought,
An illusion, in the mind's web caught?
The nature of consciousness, a mystery deep,
In its depths, the secrets of the universe sleep.
Exploring these corridors, we seek to find,
The nature of reality, through the mirrors of the mind.

Voyage of the Soul

In the quiet night, under the watchful gaze of the cosmos,
The soul embarks on its greatest voyage,
A journey not across the vastness of space,
But into the depths of its own essence.
Seeking meaning in the tapestry of existence,
Where every thread is a question,
And every color a possible answer.
In this pursuit, the soul finds its purpose,
Not in the destination, but in the journey itself,
A voyage that spans the breadth of life,
Guided by the stars of hope, love, and wisdom.

The Seeker's Song

With a heart heavy with questions,
The seeker walks the path of life,
Footsteps echoing in the silence of the universe,
A melody of longing for understanding.
Each step, a verse in the song of existence,
Sung in the key of curiosity and wonder.
In the chorus, a refrain of purpose and meaning,
Found in the simple acts of kindness,
In the pursuit of passions,
And in the connections that bind us all.
The seeker's song, a hymn to the beauty of the quest,
For meaning in a world that often seems indifferent.

Canvas of Existence

Life, a canvas vast and unfathomable,
Upon which we paint our quests for meaning.
With strokes of experiences, emotions, and thoughts,
We create a masterpiece unique to each soul.
Searching for purpose in the hues of our actions,
And in the shadows of our doubts and fears.
The palette of existence, rich with the colors of possibilities,
Invites us to paint our own paths to fulfillment,
Discovering meaning not in the echoes of the universe,
But in the silence of our inner worlds.

The Architect of Meaning

In the architecture of existence,
We are both the builders and the dwellings,
Crafting meaning with the tools of our beliefs and values.
Each brick laid with the mortar of our experiences,
Each room echoing with the laughter and tears of our journeys.
The design, uniquely our own,
Reflects the complexity of our quest for purpose.
In this structure of life,
We find shelter from the chaos of the universe,
A home where meaning resides,
Built with the hands of our own understanding.

Ephemeral Echoes

In the whispering winds of time,
Echoes of our quest for meaning travel,
Ephemeral and fleeting, like the mist at dawn.
We chase these whispers,
Grasping at the secrets they hold,
Seeking to understand the purpose of our existence.
In the silence that follows the echo,
In the stillness that comes after the search,
We find that meaning lies not in the echoes themselves,
But in our willingness to listen,
And in the courage to continue the quest,
Even when the answers seem just out of reach.

The Scales of Justice

In the hallowed halls of thought and reason,
Where the scales of justice delicately teeter,
Lies the essence of ethics, the balance of right,
A perpetual quest in humanity's plight.
Between societal norms and the heart's silent plea,
We navigate the waters of morality.
For in each decision, a whisper of virtue,
A test of our principles, steadfast and true.
May we seek not just the good life for our own,
But a world where justice and kindness are sown.

The Crossroads

At the crossroads of existence, under the gaze of the
moral compass,
We stand, contemplative, our souls amidst a tempest.
Here, personal beliefs and societal dictates clash,
Sparking the flames of ethical dilemmas,
a luminescent flash.
In this tension, a question, echoing deep and wide,
"How shall we live?" it asks, a challenge to our pride.
For at this junction, our values are our guide,
Leading us on the path where integrity resides.

The Tapestry of Morality

Life, a tapestry woven with threads of moral choice,
Each hue a decision, each pattern a voice.
Within this fabric, the stories of right and wrong intertwine,
Revealing the complexity of the ethical design.
What is virtue, but the courage to stand for what's just?
And morality, but the trust in the heart's robust?
In this woven narrative, let us find the grace,
To weave our actions with compassion and embrace.

Echoes of Virtue

In the quiet moments, virtue whispers, soft and clear,
A gentle reminder of what we hold dear.
Beyond the clamor of the world's demanding cries,
Lies the truth of what it means to be wise.
For wisdom is not merely knowledge, but the application,
Of ethics and morals in every situation.
May our echoes of virtue ring true and resonate,
Guiding us to live lives that goodness and truth
celebrate.

The Guardian of the Good

In the garden of life, where choices bloom and fade,
Stands the guardian of the good, beneath the wisdom's shade.
With a gaze that pierces through the veil of right and wrong,
It guards the gate to a life where virtues belong.
This guardian, not of stone, but of flesh and thought,
Reminds us that morality cannot be bought.
But nurtured in the soul, through actions kind and just,
In the garden of ethics, in the guardian, we trust.

The River of Time

Time flows like a river, relentless and serene,
Carrying us forward, to places unseen.
Its waters, deep with memories, swirl and churn,
Echoes of the past, from which we yearn to learn.
Yet, in its current, we find the essence of our tale,
A journey of moments, fleeting and frail.
For in the river of time, we see our reflection,
A mosaic of life, in its fleeting perfection.

The Tapestry of Memory

Woven into the fabric of our being, memory resides,
A tapestry rich with color, where the past abides.
Each thread, a remembrance, intricately spun,
Telling tales of battles lost, of victories won.
This fabric of our identity, shaped by each recall,
Holds the power to uplift us, or to make us fall.
Yet, in its weave, the strength of the human spirit,
A testament to our capacity to endure, to inherit.

Shadows of the Future

In the shadows of the future, where time stretches wide,
Lies the realm of possibility, with fate as our guide.
A landscape uncharted, veiled in misty doubt,
Where dreams take flight, and hopes sprout.
Yet, in this uncertainty, a beauty so profound,
For in the quest for tomorrow, our true selves are found.
Embracing the unknown, we step into the light,
Carving paths through time, with futures bright.

The Clockwork of Existence

Tick-tock, the clockwork of existence beats,
A rhythm of life, where past and future meets.
Each tick, a moment; each tock, a sigh,
In the dance of time, where moments fly.
But within this clockwork, a silence profound,
A space for reflection, where meaning is found.
For in the ticking away of our earthly hours,
Lies the power to blossom, to unfold like flowers.

Elegy to Memory

An elegy to memory, to the echoes of the past,
To the moments captured, too beautiful to last.
In the heart's recesses, where these memories dwell,
A story of who we are, a tale they tell.
Yet, with each passing year, some fade into the mist,
Leaving behind shadows, by time's gentle twist.
But let us not mourn the memories that wane,
For in their fleeting, our identities remain.

Mirrors and Windows

In the realm of consciousness,
where self and otherness blend,
We stand before mirrors and windows,
on perceptions they depend.
Mirrors reflecting the depths within,
revealing our own face,
Windows offering glimpses of the world,
a vast, interconnected space.
The self, a unique constellation of thoughts,
dreams, and fears,
Yet linked to the 'other,'
through the lens of empathy, it peers.
In this dance of individuality and unity,
We discover the illusion of separateness, the
truth of community.

The Tapestry of Being

We are threads in the tapestry of being,
each a vibrant hue,
Our colors distinct, yet interwoven, creating a view
Of a world rich with diversity, complexity, and grace,
Where the self meets the other, in time and space.
This fabric of existence,
where identities merge and flow,
Teaches us that in the 'other,'
parts of ourselves we come to know.
For in the reflection of the world's wide eyes,
We find our own essence, and in understanding,
become wise.

The Bridge Between

Between the self and the 'other,'
a bridge spans wide,
Built from the stones of empathy,
understanding, and pride.
Crossing this expanse,
we journey from the known to the new,
Discovering that in the heart of the 'other,'
truths reside, deep and true.
This bridge,
a conduit for shared experiences and dreams,
Reminds us that the world is
more connected than it seems.
For in the meeting of minds and merging of souls,
We find our common humanity,
the part that makes us whole.

Echoes of the Self

In the echoes of the self, where thoughts and feelings reside,
Lies the essence of our being, the core of our pride.
Yet, these echoes do not sound in isolation or in vain,
For they reverberate in the hearts of others, a shared refrain.
The 'other,' once perceived as distant, foreign, or unknown,
Becomes a mirror reflecting our own tone.
In this resonance of the self with the world outside,
We discover our interconnectedness, a truth we cannot hide.

The Illusion of Separateness

The illusion of separateness, a veil over our eyes,
Obscures the truth of our interconnectedness, the ties
That bind us to each other, to the earth, and to the sky,
A network of existence, where our spirits fly.
The self, a drop in the ocean of the vast universe,
Finds in the 'other,' a universe diverse.
Breaking through the illusion, we come to see
That in our shared being lies our true identity.

The First Step

In the quiet before dawn, where self-doubt once lay,
I took the first step, at the break of day.
A path unworn, through the thicket of fear,
Where the voice of self-love began to draw near.
Each stride, a battle; each breath, a fight,
Against the shadows cast by the night.
But in the struggle, a light began to shine,
Illuminating the journey to claiming what's mine.
Self-acceptance, the destination, long sought,
In the battles of the mind, bravely fought.

Mirror's Truth

Before a mirror, I stood, eyes locked in gaze,
Confronting the reflection of my own maze.
The mirror whispered, through glass and frame,
"See not just flaws, but your inner flame."
With every glance, a revelation,
Of self-love's quiet, steady foundation.
No longer a critic, but a friend reflected,
In the mirror's truth, I stood, connected.
A hurdle overcome, in the heart's deep dive,
Finding love for oneself, truly alive.

The Garden Within

In the garden within, where doubts used to grow,
I planted seeds of self-love, and watched them sow.
Through soil of fear and under skies of pain,
Sprouted blooms of acceptance, in sunshine and rain.
Each petal, a lesson; each color, a dream,
In the garden of self, a newfound esteem.
Tending to love, with care and with grace,
In the heart's fertile ground, found a sacred space.
Where once there were thorns, now flowers reside,
In the garden within, where self-love abides.

The Climb

A mountain stood, daunting, in the terrain of the mind,
Its peak shrouded in mist, its paths unkind.
Self-doubt, the mountain; self-love, the peak,
The journey to the summit, a quest to seek.
With each step upward, the climb grew steep,
But the resolve for self-love was a vow to keep.
At the pinnacle, breathless, looking down at the trail,
Realized the strength within, that could never fail.
The hurdles overcome, on this rugged climb,
Revealed the power of self-love, sublime.

Rivers of Reflection

Through rivers of reflection, I sailed my boat,
Over waters of doubt, barely afloat.
Each wave, a fear; each ripple, a tear,
In the journey to self-love, I steered near.
Navigating through storms of self-reproach,
To shores of acceptance, I approached.
With the compass of compassion, I found my way,
To the oceans of self-love, bright as day.
The journey long, with hurdles past,
Led to the haven of self-love, vast.

I Am Enough

In the stillness of dawn, let this truth resonate,
"I am enough," a mantra to state.
Not as a whisper, but loud and clear,
For the heart to absorb, for the soul to hear.
In every fiber, in every breath,
This affirmation against doubt and death.
I am enough, with all my flaws and grace,
A unique being, in time and space.

The Light Within

There's a light within me, bright and strong,
An eternal flame, where I belong.
It shines through darkness, through fear and pain,
A reminder of my worth, again and again.
This light, my guide, my beacon, my song,
Tells me I'm valuable, right where I belong.
So, in moments of doubt, this truth I will hold,
The light within me, precious and bold.

Roots of Strength

Deep within, my roots grow wide and deep,
Anchored in the earth, a strength to keep.
From these roots, my worth does bloom,
Rising above, dispelling gloom.
This strength, a testament to my journey long,
A foundation of worth, unshakeable and strong.
Let me not forget, in storm or in drought,
The depth of my value, inside and out.

Waves of Grace

Like the ocean, my worth ebbs and flows,
In waves of grace, it freely goes.
Each crest, a peak of my unique qualities,
Each trough, a moment to gather new energies.
Boundless and vast, my worth does extend,
Beyond horizons, without end.
In the rhythm of the sea, let me find,
The infinite worth of my own mind.

Stars of Uniqueness

In the tapestry of night, each star a story tells,
Of uniqueness and beauty, in vast celestial wells.
So too am I, a star in the human sea,
Shining with worth, vibrant and free.
My light, distinct, a hue of its own,
A piece of the cosmos, into existence sown.
May I remember, when shadows cast their night,
My inherent worth, my unique light.

Against the Storm

In the heart of the tempest, where winds roar and rain falls,
Stands a spirit, unbowed, amidst the tumultuous calls.
For every lightning strike, a resolve stronger,
With each thunder clap, their heart beats longer.
This resilience, a testament to the soul's might,
A beacon of hope in the darkest night.
Emerging from the storm, not unscathed but alive,
A story of overcoming, a will to survive.

The Phoenix's Rebirth

From the ashes of despair, a phoenix rises,
Wings spread wide, it symbolizes
The power of renewal, the strength to begin anew,
A journey through fire, to find what's true.
This resilience, a fire burning bright within,
A force of nature, a fight to win.
Out of adversity, a new self emerges,
On the wings of resilience, the spirit surges.

Rivers of Healing

Gentle rivers of healing, through the soul they wind,
Carving paths of peace, leaving pain behind.
These waters, soothing, a balm to the weary heart,
Teach us that from our struggles, we can part.
Resilience, not in hardening, but in the flow,
Finding strength in vulnerability,
allowing healing to grow.
Through adversity, these rivers carve a way,
Leading to the dawn of a brighter day.

Mountains of Resolve

Like mountains standing tall against
the sky's vast expanse,
So too does the human spirit,
against adversity advance.
Each peak, a challenge overcome,
each valley, a lesson learned,
In the landscape of resilience,
these victories are earned.
With every step upward, a testament to strength,
A journey of endurance, of untold length.
This resolve, a force that can bend but never break,
In the heart of the resilient, a steadfast quake.

The Warrior's Whisper

There's a whisper in the heart of every warrior,
fighting their unseen fight,
A soft murmur of resilience,
in the quiet of the night.
It speaks of battles won and lost,
of scars worn with pride,
Of the strength found in moments when
they thought they'd died.
This whisper, a reminder of the power within,
The resilience of the spirit, a light that never dims.
In the silence, listen closely, and you may hear
The warrior's whisper, "Persevere, persevere."

Unveiling

In the quiet spaces between our breaths,
Lies the unspoken truth of our essence.
Vulnerability, not a weakness but a bridge,
Connecting the islands of our solitude.
Here, in the unveiling of our deepest fears,
We discover the paradoxical strength of being seen,
Raw and unadorned,
A testament to the courage it takes
To stand in the light of our own truth.

The Dance of Shadows

Life invites us to a dance, a delicate balance
Between light and shadow,
Where vulnerability leads the steps.
It is in this dance that we shed the layers,
The masks and armors worn too long.
With each step, a revelation,
That the power we sought through concealment
Flourishes in the open wounds we dare to show.
A dance where authenticity breathes,
And in its breath, we find freedom.

Walls Crumble

There are walls we build, stone by stone,
Around our hearts, a fortress to protect the softness within.
Yet, in the silent acknowledgment of our vulnerabilities,
These walls do not weaken but crumble,
Revealing not the fragility we feared,
But a profound strength in openness.
For it is in the moments of our greatest exposures
That we invite connections most genuine,
A strength that flourishes in the soil of authenticity.

The Gift of Tears

Tears, often seen as the language of the weak,
Are instead the expressions of a strength untold.
In our vulnerabilities, when tears freely flow,
We offer the world a gift,
The beauty of unguarded emotion,
A display of the complex tapestry
that is the human soul.
Embracing these moments of raw tenderness,
We acknowledge the power inherent
in our truest selves,
A force that thrives not in hiding,
but in the honesty of our pain.

Echoes of Authenticity

In the echoes of our authenticity,
Where vulnerability speaks louder than words,
There lies a strength unforeseen.
It is a journey inward, to the depths where fear resides,
To greet it, to know it, and to let it go.
In this space, where pretense falls away,
We meet the essence of our true selves,
A strength that does not roar but whispers,
Reminding us that in our openness,
We are unbreakable, boundless, and free.

The Uncharted Path

There is a path that winds deep within,
where footprints of the past and
the shadows of the future
merge into the journey of now.
This path, unmarked by the signs of societal expectation,
invites the traveler to wander, to question,
to peel away the layers of labels and roles
until the core is reached.
Here, in the solitude of self-discovery,
one finds the essence of identity,
not bestowed or borrowed,
but birthed from the depths of personal truth.

Reflections in the Water

Imagine staring into a still pond,
the surface a mirror to the sky, the trees,
the world upside down.
But deeper still, beneath the reflection, lies clarity,
a vision of the self beyond the mirrored sky.
In this quest for identity,
we dive beneath the surface of what the world expects,
finding in the cool depths the shapes and colors
of our most authentic selves.
This reflection, not of the world, but of the soul,
reveals the vibrant hues of individuality,
a spectrum of being uniquely our own.

The Conversation Within

There is a conversation that happens in the
quiet spaces of the mind,
where voices of doubt and dreams of becoming
entwine in a dialogue of discovery.
This internal discourse, unfiltered by the
ears of others,
is where one asks and answers the most
intimate questions of being.
Who am I in the absence of the world’s gaze?
What truths lie beneath the roles I play?
In this conversation, a narrative unfolds,
a story of self that is continuously being
written
in the ink of experience and the paper of
existence.

Layers

Like geological strata bearing the
imprints of eras gone by,
our selves are composed of layers,
each one a chapter in the saga of becoming.
Peeling these layers does not weaken the structure,
but reveals the complexity of our identity,
rich with the fossils of past selves,
the sediment of experiences,
and the minerals of dreams yet crystallized.
In this excavation of self, we discover not
a singular essence
but a mosaic of being,
each piece a testament to the journey of discovery.

The Map of Me

Consider a map not drawn by cartographers,
but by the wandering of one's own steps,
a chart where roads are made not of asphalt but of choices,
and landmarks are moments of revelation rather than monuments.
On this map, the journey of self-discovery traces routes
through terrains of joy and valleys of challenge,
each turn a decision, each destination a discovery.
Here, the compass points not north, but inward,
guiding the traveler to the most sacred destination:
the heart of their identity,
a place where the true self resides,
waiting to be found and celebrated.

The Seasons Within

There is a seasonality to our being,
cycles of change that mirror the world outside.
Just as winter gives way to spring,
so too do our inner landscapes transform.
The inevitability of change is not a harbinger of loss,
but a promise of renewal and growth.
Embracing these shifts with an open heart,
we allow ourselves to blossom,
shedding old leaves to make way for new growth,
a perpetual rebirth of the self in the face of change.

Tides of Transformation

Life moves in tides, a constant flow of coming and going,
where change is the only true constant.
Each wave that retreats leaves the shore altered,
just as each experience reshapes the contours of our selves.
To stand against the tide is to deny the essence of existence,
but to move with it, to embrace the ebb and flow,
is to understand the beauty of transformation.
In this acceptance, we find strength,
not in the permanence of sandcastles,
but in the fluidity of the water that shapes them.

The Metamorphosis

Consider the caterpillar, ensconced in its cocoon,
a creature of the earth bound for the sky.
The process of metamorphosis, so intrinsic to nature,
is also intrinsic to us.
Each phase of our lives demands a shedding of old skins,
a preparation for the wings we are yet to unfold.
Embracing change is embracing the potential for flight,
an acceptance of the beauty in transformation,
and the courage to emerge, time and again,
renewed and ready for the open air.

Crossroads

At the crossroads of our lives, we stand,
facing the myriad paths that stretch before us.
Change beckons from each direction,
a call to journey into the unknown.
These junctions, though fraught with uncertainty,
are also brimming with potential.
To choose a path is to embrace change,
to acknowledge that growth lies not
in the safety of the known,
but in the challenge of the unfamiliar.
With each step forward, we chart a course of becoming,
a testament to the power of an open heart.

The Sculptor

Life, the sculptor, works in the medium of change,
chiseling away at the marble of our existence.
Each strike, a transformation; each chip, a revelation.
Though the process may unsettle,
what emerges is a form more true to itself than before.
Embracing change is to embrace the sculptor’s vision,
to see the beauty in the making,
and to trust in the artwork that we are becoming.
In this trust, we find not just acceptance,
but a celebration of the masterpiece in progress,
a life shaped by the loving hands of change.

The Forge of Will

In the forge of will, where determination glows hot,
a vision is hammered into existence.
This place is not found on any map,
but within the boundless landscapes of the self.
Here, courage is the anvil, and action the hammer,
shaping dreams into reality
with every determined strike.
To stand in this forge is to
embrace the heat of potential,
to understand that within the heart
lies the power to mold the world.
The path to self-empowerment begins
with a single step,
a step taken with the full weight of belief
in one's own strength,
a belief that says,
"I am the architect of my destiny,
the sculptor of my dreams,
and the author of my journey."

The Beacon of Purpose

There is a beacon within, radiating purpose,
a light that guides through the darkest
nights and the fiercest storms.
This light is fed by the flames
of passion and the fuel of dreams,
illuminating the path to self-empowerment.
To follow this light is to walk a road paved
with challenges,
yet each obstacle overcome is a testament to the
resilience of the spirit.
With every step forward, the light grows brighter,
casting away doubts and fears, revealing the strength
that lies within.
This journey is not for the faint of heart,
but for those who dare to dream, to act, and to achieve.
The beacon of purpose shines not just as a guide,
but as a reminder that within us all is the power to
illuminate the world.

Wings of Change

On the wings of change, we soar,
embracing the winds of possibility that lift us
to new heights.
These wings are not given but made,
crafted from the fabric of our convictions and
the threads of our aspirations.
To fly is to acknowledge the vastness of the sky,
and to know that it is not the domain of the birds alone,
but of any who possess the courage to leap.
The path to self-empowerment is both
a flight and a journey,
a journey that begins with the belief
in one's ability to rise,
to ascend beyond the limits of the past and the
constraints of the present.
With these wings, we chart our own course,
not as passengers of fate, but as pilots of our destiny,
guided by the belief that within us lies the power to
change not only our lives
but the very course of the world itself.

The Art of Letting Go

In the quiet chambers of the heart,
where guilt and regret like shadows linger,
there is an art to letting go,
a delicate process of untying the knots of self-blame.
This is where the wisdom of self-forgiveness whispers,
softly, persistently,
that mistakes are not chains to bind us
but lessons to guide us.
To forgive oneself is to acknowledge the
flaw in our design,
the imperfection that makes us human.
And in this acknowledgment, there is freedom,
a release that allows us to step forward,
not unscarred, but enlightened,
carrying the knowledge of our errors
as lanterns to light the path of growth.

Compassion's Journey

The journey inward is the longest trek,
a path fraught with the debris of past missteps.
Each one a reminder of moments when we faltered,
when the weight of our actions lay heavy on our soul.
Yet, it is here, in the depths of introspection,
that the seed of self-forgiveness is found.
To water this seed is an act of compassion,
a recognition that to err is intrinsic to our nature.
With gentle hands, we must tend to our wounds,
understanding that forgiveness is not an erasure
but an acceptance,
a way to embrace our entire selves,
flaws and all,
and in doing so, find a way to move forward,
not anchored by the past, but buoyed by the wisdom
it has imparted.

Bridges to Tomorrow

Mistakes, like stones in a river,
can hinder our flow,
catching us in the eddies of regret and self-doubt.
Self-forgiveness is the bridge over these waters,
a structure built from the timber of
understanding and grace.
Crossing this bridge requires courage,
the strength to accept our imperfections
and the resolve to learn from them.
On the other side lies a landscape of possibilities,
a horizon not defined by the errors of yesterday
but shaped by the wisdom of today.
To forgive oneself is to grant permission to grow,
to evolve beyond the confines of past judgments
and step into the vastness of our potential,
with hearts open to the lessons of life
and eyes fixed on the promise of the future.

Reflections in Still Waters

In the stillness of a mountain lake,
the surface mirrors the sky,
a perfect reflection of the world above.
So too does the soul reflect
the beauty and depth within,
a reminder that tranquility and clarity
come from embracing the stillness of our own nature.

Seasons of the Self

Just as the earth cycles through seasons,
so do we.
Winter's retreat and spring's bloom
mirror our own periods of dormancy and growth.
With each cycle, a reminder:
what lies dormant will always awaken,
and what blooms will surely thrive,
a testament to the resilience and renewal
inherent in both nature and ourselves.

The Mountain's Lesson

The mountain stands, immovable,
a testament to time and endurance.
Its peaks, reaching for the heavens,
teach us to stand tall in our truth,
to endure through storms and sun alike,
and to remember that our strength
is as much a part of us
as it is of the mountain's ancient stone.
In its presence, we see a mirror,
reflecting the enduring beauty and resilience
of our own nature.

Uncharted Paths

In the vast expanse of existence,
each soul charts its own unmarked path.
Footsteps, not in tandem but in rhythm
with the heart's unique beat.
This journey, a tapestry of quirks and questions,
weaves a story not of conformity,
but of vivid hues of individuality.
Let us celebrate each twist, each turn,
for in the divergence lies the true adventure,
a declaration of self in a world of sameness.

The Symphony of Self

Life, a symphony with a billion melodies,
each note played on the strings of individuality.
Your song, distinct amidst the chorus,
carries the weight of your essence,
a melody composed of quirks, dreams, and desires.
To mute this melody is to dim the world's vibrance.
So play on, let the notes of your unique song
fill the air with the music of being
unapologetically you.

Kaleidoscope Being

A kaleidoscope, ever-shifting, ever-changing,
mirrors the essence of our being.
Each turn, a new pattern of colors,
a fresh perspective on the same set of shapes.
Your quirks, the colors; your interests, the shapes,
together, creating patterns no one else can replicate.
In this celebration of individuality,
we find the beauty in variation,
the strength in difference,
a world kaleidoscopically rich
with the irreplaceable and the incomparable you.

Winds of Change

In the heart of the night, under the moon's soft glow,
Lies the courage to release, to finally let go.
Of bonds that bind, of chains that hold,
Of stories untold, of dreams sold.
The winds of change whisper, soft and low,
"It's time to leave behind what you've outgrown."
With every step forward, away from the past,
We find our true selves, free at last.

Shedding Skins

Like a snake sheds its skin, so must we,
Release the old, to let the new be.
Layers of doubt, fear, and woe,
Must be cast off, for growth to show.
In the act of letting go, we find release,
A sense of peace, a feeling of ease.
For in the space where once doubts crept,
Lies new strength, our promises kept.

Unfettered Flight

Bound by chains of our own creation,
We seek liberation, a new foundation.
Toxic ties that once felt like home,
We now discern, through our growth, we've outgrown.
With wings unfurled, into the skies we soar,
Leaving behind what we no longer adore.
In the art of letting go, we find our might,
Emerging from shadows into the light.

Beyond the Bounds

In the quiet heart of night, where truths are known,
Lies the strength to walk paths, once shown.
To let go of chains, once tightly bound,
In their release, our true selves found.
Shedding the weight of yesteryears' hold,
Embracing the new, letting the old fold.
The art of release, a dance, a song,
Moving forward, where we truly belong.

Echoes Fade

Once whispered promises, now echoes fade,
In the art of letting go, our peace is made.
Releasing the grip of what was meant to be,
Setting our hearts and our futures free.
Unrealistic hopes, like leaves, drift away,
Making room for the new in the light of day.
In the space that's left, growth takes its stand,
On the fresh soil of an unburdened land.

Wings Unfurled

Beneath the layers of doubt and fear,
Lies a soul unbound, crystal clear.
Letting go of the masks we've worn so tight,
Revealing our essence, pure and bright.
With wings unfurled, into the sky, we leap,
Beyond the cliffs of limitations steep.
In the art of release, we find our flight,
Soaring into our dreams, into the light.

Now Is the Key

In this moment, the world unfolds anew,
The past a whisper, the future's hue
Fades into the backdrop of the now,
Where every breath teaches us how
To embrace the present, with all its light,
Shadows dispelled by mindfulness bright.
Each second a gift, unwrapped with care,
In the art of presence, we find what's truly rare.

The Dance of the Present

With each step taken, feel the ground,
The rhythm of life, in the moment found.
Not ahead nor behind, but in the dance of the now,
Mindfulness leads, to its beat we bow.
This path we walk, a journey of grace,
Each footprint a memory, time cannot erase.
In the heart of the present, our worries cease,
In the embrace of the moment, we find our peace.

Stream of Being

Like a stream that flows, serene and clear,
Mindfulness washes away the fear.
In the babble of the brook, the present's voice,
Calls us to rejoice, to make the choice
To live in this instant, where life is keen,
To see the beauty in spaces between.
The practice of being, simple and profound,
In the art of the moment, our selves are found.

Thank you for journeying through these pages. Your engagement with this collection is deeply appreciated, and we hope it has offered you moments of reflection, insight, and perhaps even transformation.

If this book has resonated with you, please consider sharing your thoughts by leaving a review on Amazon. Your feedback is invaluable, helping others discover and explore these poems.

Additionally, we invite you to join our community on TikTok for more inspiration and connection with like-minded souls.

Your support means the world to us. Thank you for being a part of this journey.

Warmly,

Talia Quell

www.ingramcontent.com/pod-product-compliance
Lightning Source LLC
Chambersburg PA
CBHW031411250726
48656CB00002B/635
9798322024200